PIE FACE

A love story about a Newfoundland in Oregon

Published   January 24, 2018

Once upon a time, in a seemingly enchanted forest covered land crisscrossed by three sparkling rivers, spanned by covered bridges; beautiful rivers that filled countless waterfalls, lived the most wonderous puppy that the residents of Eugene had ever known.

It seems that the most heartwarming stories are fairytales that thrive for generations and centuries, oftentimes of the larger than life and times of a Princess or Dragon. And it seems that most are fables written to lighten the heart and are known to be mostly fictional figments of an optimistic, fertile imagination. Such readers of this fiction follow the writer's thoughts and bring to life such stories when they dream.

And it seems that these dragon stories must begin with "Once upon a time..."

The story of Pie Face began about fifteen years before he was born. His name came from the shared imagination of his soon to be adopting parents Christina and Gene Constant. We lived in Southern California at that time, where we yearned for the day when we could live in a place where big dogs could be a part of our family.

I have always been an avid reader of the Marmaduke comic strip, which is about a happy Great Dane, and we were frequent patrons of a regionally famous café/bakery known as Baker's Square. The creator of Marmaduke oftentimes invited readers to submit a short story about their dog, stories that could be included in the last box of the Sunday comic edition. While dining, we wrote a story of a puppy who loved pie so much that there seemed to always be a bit of whipped cream remaining on his nose until the very last lick.

We were thrilled to see that the story of our fictional pup was published, and it was agreed that if we were to be so fortunate as to share a life with a giant dog, that his name would be Pie Face.

The opportunity to fulfill our doggie dreams came to fruition when we moved our online uniform apparel business from Riverside California to Eugene Oregon in late June 2008, where we added a retail store. It was our good fortune to have obtained a lease of a 2,300-sq. ft. home situated on eight wooded acres from Grant, big-hearted gentleman who almost instantly became a very close friend.

He understood our puppy craving and very soon after our arrival, he agreed to our request for permission to adopt & raise a Newfoundland puppy.

Available for sale at Amazon.com

And what a wonderful place to raise a puppy! The woods were alive with deer that were so tame, they would sleep next to the house and walk right up onto the porch. We also enjoyed the frequent company of turkeys, racoon and thumbnail sized frogs.

In no time at all, we found a horse & Newfoundland breeder in Missouri who was soon to be blessed with a litter of Newfie pups, and the rest is history. They emailed us these images of our soon-to-be son when he was about four weeks old, and of course we instantly fell in love with this little fur ball.

Our newly adopted baby boy flew to the Portland Oregon airport, where I picked him up around May 22, 2009. He was a bit shy at first, and soon adjusted to me and his first car ride quite fine. I had initially placed him onto his first (and last) baby bed on the front passenger floorboard with a bit of food & water, which he sampled. Within 20 minutes or so, he had climbed into the passenger seat of my new 2009 Pontiac GT pearl white convertible. Seconds later we started bonding as he walked onto my lap and eventually placed his front paws on the edge of the driver's door for his first taste of Oregon breeze.

He was forever addicted to that fresh fir-tree cleaned Oregon breeze, and acted so whenever he heard the words "car ride". He would signal his desire for me get that window down by pressing his nose to the glass. As the window dropped, he would quickly stick that massive head outside the car for some of that Oregon-fresh nose candy.

Pie Face had a lot of fun talking to turkeys. He would bark at them from the porches (this home is surrounded by porch and every room has a sliding glass door to it). On two occasions he lazily chased the turkeys until they effortlessly flew to the trees, as they would then look down at this happy pup. He also gave chase to the deer, but they would bounce away and over the 5-ft. fence surrounding the property. The turkeys would talk to him regularly from the tree line, singing their "gobble gobble" noise, whereupon Pie Face would answer with several barks, etc. until their chats concluded. His tail wagged like a fly swatter as he obviously took great delight in the verbal exchange. 😊

Welcome to your new home little man!

Christina and I married in 1987 at the youthful age of 35, neither of us had children before or since, and

both of us had zero experience with infant behavior of any kind for any reason. We knew there would be a lot of trial & error, being both teacher & student in our new family. A puppy has many similarities to that of child rearing, including potty training, communication, family & public behavior and diet. For the puppy, he must deal with understanding how to interface with a different species. You must admire one of God's creatures who come into a world in which they cannot ever speak the language, nor use many of the tools and furniture that their new mom & dad seem comfortable with.

Where to sleep: using the internet to search for help, it seemed important for puppies to sleep outside. I took Pie Face's new baby bed and placed it and him on one of the porches, after securing the only avenue of escape or adventure with temporary fence.

Pie Face set some ground rules of his own right away about his desired sleeping arrangements. He scratched the glass door and whined tirelessly, telling us that he would not allow any separation in his new home. That little guy can make a very loud noise!

Plan B: we purchased a gate used for babies to close off a ½ bath that was near the kitchen, allowing him visibility down the long hallway to all the rest of the house. This bath was near the entertainment area and front room. This bath location gave Pie Face a large space to hang out, while the linoleum flood helped to minimize stains that would occur before his potty training.

Neither one of us could imaging wanting, nor puppy allowing the use of a cage for training. Our baby accepted this compromise and that is how things remained for about one month, as this very smart guy quickly proved a quick learner at asking to go outdoors when nature called. Pie Face demonstrated his desire to be with us that very first day of his arrival.

He continued to make a fuss over the baby gate, and proved when given the opportunity that he could be trusted. Pie also demonstrated a strong need for the exchange of affection, proving to us that he had a lot of love to give at every opportunity.

<u>Where to eat:</u> we did try feeding him outside the kitchen door where we placed a water & food dish. He did his best to cooperate with that arrangement as he quickly proved to be a foodie. His excitement during meal time seemed to present a challenge the previous family had not encountered, and that was the four-foot drop from the porch. Such as fall to someone so small could lead to injury or worst, so we moved his dishes to the kitchen.

What we found stunning was just how FAST he was growing, rocking two pair of very long legs. And it seemed almost like a thing you may see on a sci-fi movie where he morphed into this big and more handsome man in a few short months.

I told Christina that we just HAD to get this picture of him on the kitchen island, as any wait may prove to be too late for us older people to pick him up.

Pie Face loves to eat ice. Thanks to Christina's choice of treats, our little guy has never had a dental problem of any kind. If he wasn't eating the ice cubes, he would play with them by grabbing one into his mouth and then tossing it into the air. Other times the cubes would get a push from a very big paw.

Toy interests: Pie Face was presented with peanut butter filled kongs, tennis balls and stuffed toys. He loved eating the peanut butter for several months, and never was a fan of "fetch". When we threw or rolled something, he gave us an expression that clearly signaled us a "you threw it – you go get it", look, which was just the funniest expression ever! So, the unused balls were donated, because we did not want him to hurt himself, should he shred & then swallow pieces of the ball.

His other toy was the lawn sprinkler water, as you can see from these photos.

Available for sale at Amazon.com

Our puppy's fascination with sprinkler water was such, that he looked forward to the prescheduled lawn watering and INSISTED oftentimes that he go outside for that drink & play time.

With that luxurious fur coat he was born with, summer heat discomfort was made easier for him to bear when we manually turned on the sprinklers, and let him romp across the front yard from sprinkler head to head, as the different watering zones turned on/off after their fifteen minutes per zone. He taught us that his favorite toy was cardboard boxes, paper and toilet paper rolls. This saved us a lot of money and helped us to shred paper for use when lighting the fireplace. One summer he must have carried over 40 pieces of firewood, one at a time and no more than one per day. How STRONG this guy was, as most people would use two hands to carry what he happily did with his mouth.

There was one funny moment when he approached a sapling, turned his head sideways and grabbed that trunk with the intent of seeing if he could pull it from the ground! He learned that that little tree wasn't going anywhere, then focused instead on finding sticks around the property. When he found a stick that caught his eye, he would mouth it, raise his head, start wagging that giant tail like fan; then trot home with that stick just as fast as I would let him, so that he could chew that stick up on the living room carpet. He was SO happy with those frequent finds!

Living in the middle of eight acres of heaven, our baby lived in relative isolation & did not have the occasion to routinely visit or have play dates with other dogs or people, apart from deliveries by UPS or FedEx.

Christina would play with the little man by starting a cardboard game, where she got him all warmed up by little tugs and turns of a cardboard box; then let him win that tug of war when the box pieces were too small to hold. Pie Face would distance himself from her and give 100% of his efforts to shredding the box until it was no more. She always made sure he had an ample pile of boxes and sheets of cardboard to attack.

Grant provided several deer antler pieces, so Pie Face would have something more lasting to bite.

Christina also took full advantage of the dining room floor, as we had not decided on what kind of dining table & chairs to buy, when he would mouth a soft chew toy and he would hang on as she would move so that he could twirl as he slid on the polished wood floors.

Newfoundland's Spring Break 2014 – Pie Face : https://www.youtube.com/watch?v=U7p2Vca1Xgk

Big Newfoundland Dogs as pets- https://www.youtube.com/watch?v=er-hTdEstol

Our Newfoundland's Birthday - https://www.youtube.com/watch?v=3zZ8YEYiMd0

<u>First bath:</u> a puppy must be at least five weeks old before having their first bath. His first bath occurred on May 24, 2009. The pictures speak for themselves.

  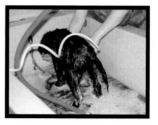 

<u>First family adventure:</u> While a picture may not be worth a thousand words, there oftentimes are not the right words to clearly express what can be said with pictures. The following images are of Pie Face's first road trip to Sweet Creek Falls near Florence Oregon in late May 2009.

First Dog park visit: Puppies teach each other about biting. Nothing makes a better teacher when needing to learn how much pressure to use when wanting to mouth people & other dogs, than to have some other dog bite your pup on the ear. Dogs need tangible examples of behavior, so a trip to play and socialize with others of the same species is a visit new dog owners must do soon and often. In these photos, our son is at Alton Baker Park near the University of Oregon Stadium.

What's a trip to a dog park if you cannot sniff a few butts!

Our son's first experience with voluntarily getting into water happened at the park that day.

I remember that moment especially well. I felt our son was uncertain of this water stuff and did not know what to do. I drained then filled, the doggie wading pool with clean water. As I was picking him up so that all four paws could touch the water at the same time, a guy standing nearby said in a cheerful voice that I should be sure of what I am getting into. He mused that this water dog may be more than a handful once the pup discovered the joy of water. How right he was.

From the wading pool, we took a bolder direction by sampling the nearby Willamette River.

Within weeks of his arrival his personality became apparent to us, as his transformation from newborn to firstborn became apparent. Strutting the porches or patrolling the unmown portions of the surrounding field, that little tough guy clearly took claim of everything he surveyed. His cocky expressions and seemingly practiced poses could only force us to smile, as our love for this gift from Heaven wiggled his way deeper and deeper into our hearts and memories.

Christina and Pie Face enjoyed the outdoor climate from which to better know each other and to facilitate training. Here are but a few of those good times.

Dining

Our son, Mr. Pie Face Constant, has always been a foodie. I define a foodie as:

1. one who seems obsessed with anything that may be considered digestible & that will not hurt too much or for too long if swallowed before it is fully chewed,
2. believes that an ingested item does not <u>have</u> to taste good to be good,
3. thinks that it is OK to marginalize #1 and #2 if there is concern that the item may be eaten by others or picked up and disposed of as trash.

To his defense, our foodie's behavior is not his fault. He can blame his doctor's orders regarding his weight. Keeping his weight down was a proactive measure to promote walking, as Newfies are prone to hip dysplasia and arthritis.

Regarding his mom, let it be known to the world that this little puppy was not born with a silver spoon in his mouth! The silver spoon was introduced by his adoptive mother AFTER he was born. She used this spoon to serve all his meals and even for a few of his snacks. A photo of exhibit A, "the silver spoon with gold plate accent" is shown on this page.

Let the

photographic evidence on this page also prove that his mother cooked most of his meals, adding human stuff like cooked hamburger, pasta and other tasty-good smelling food to his special dog food which may have acted more like a narcotic to our heretofore innocent baby boy. These pictures are graphic and may disturb other pets who are not fed by hand, with food being constantly mixed in the bowl while eating, using his own dinner plates instead of a dog dish, etc.

Pie Face's dining experiences were often enhanced by using plates instead of a doggie bowl, by having a custom-made table or by eating in the tv or other rooms. 😊

Available for sale at Amazon.com

Sometimes when Pie Face thought nobody was looking, he took it upon himself to make sure that the kitchen counters were clean.

As his dad, I admit to participating in nursing his foodie addiction as I am the one who brought home a grill. Another phrase that would catch his full attention is the word "bar b cue". Once he knew that we were serious about cooking outside, he was all in, waiting patiently (or not so much), guarding the grill from potential squirrels or other imagined competitors.

Ricardo measured Pie Face and crafted this solid oak table, with the raised edges to prevent an excited dog from pushing his dish off a flat surface; and the curved legs for style. In this picture you can see the mixing bowl where I made mashed potatoes (he LOVES mashed potatoes) and that Christina has blended my cooking into our son's dog food.

SLEEPING ACCOMODATIONS

Our little bundle of joy chewed up his baby bed within his first three months, as if it were nothing more than a box. I saw his effort as a demand for a bigger bed. His second bed included embroidery of his name, and he used it until it was too worn out to suit him two years later.

My baby boy had a practice of wanting to share, that if it was good enough for you, then he would have to give it a try too.

From the next photos you will find him napping or resting on my new recliner & patio lounging chair. For the life of me I never figured out how he was able to muster the dexterity to pull those long legs OUT of that patio lounge chair!

Mr. Pie Face Constant quickly became the sole occupant of an Italian leather couch that was given to us by Christina's mother soon after we were married. We also installed an embroidered liner for the back seat of our car, as he had a sensitive tummy and would throw-up on some car rides.

By Gene Constant

First Family Portrait

I have been taking photos for all my adult life. It seemed to be a simple matter of getting our child to sit down for our first family photo. to celebrate our son's first birthday. After all, I have photographed dogs, cats, horses and hundreds of weddings. Piece of cake! Right?

Wrong.

No kind of food nor amount of begging could change Pie Face's greater want to be with me, or to study the camera/tripod. He was just full of puppy energy and curiosity. We did get pleasing portraits of mom & son individually with this fur ball. The family portrait was accomplished via a paid photoshoot at Petco near the River Valley Mall in Eugene. Some months later, Christina took the picture you see above of dad & son in the front of my "boat".

First Snow

Newfoundlands are very well known for their instinct to rescue people who seem to be having trouble in the water, as nanny dogs who LOVE children, and for working in very wintry conditions such as snow.

We moved to Eugene Oregon because we were convinced that this portion of beautiful land would have almost no snow. The fact that Eugene does not have one snow plow seemed proof of that belief.

It less a surprise so much of a SHOCK that we found all this WHITE stuff outdoors in early 2012. While waiting for it to melt, our baby was only too happy to have the temporary resting place to nest.

From the arrival of Pie Face in late May 2009 until our move to a more modest apartment in April 2015, we three learned a lot about each other. That learning became a life which morphed into a love that I had never experienced before.

I had never known what unconditional love was, nor did I ever imagine of such an opportunity. Yet here I was living a dream that only a pet can give. When I came home from work, Christina would open the kitchen door after I had parked my car and this four-legged bundle of joy would run to me, then jump and run around me. Then we would walk, talk & touch from the driveway to the kitchen, and begin an evening of bonding & sharing. Had I known such a feeling was possible, I would have been a parent to a dog a very long time ago. In the first six years puppy & I had been together (I cannot speak for Christina about this thought), I discovered a brother, a friend, a confidant, a son and a love beyond that of which can be found with a human being. I truly believe that this world would be a much better place if we humans could only learn from our dogs. I am also convinced that GOD made dogs to be man's best friend for a purpose. If we could only get our heads around this.

Before we begin sharing our experiences as apartment dwellers, I wish to share a few images that I could not pigeonhole into a category but give me so many great vibes.

July 11, 2014

Available for sale at Amazon.com

PIE FACE – A love story about a Newfoundland in Oregon

Heaven
on Earth

Transition

Pie Face found the move to apartment living to be nothing less than Heaven on Earth.

Before the move, I would best describe our puppy as one who far exceeded our expectations, as to what it would be like to adopt and raise a pet. By every measure, Pie Face found loving and caring parents when he arrived in Oregon. Affection and devotion was aplenty from all three parties in this family. It is no exaggeration when I candidly say that we three were and shall always be in love with each other.

Most would say that in such a circumstance, what more could you ask for? I was satisfied right down to the bone, to be sure!

Then we moved to an apartment.

Our Newfie literally transformed overnight, acquiring a seemingly overdeveloped sense of purpose, paired with a surprisingly stunning larger-than-life personality. I rapidly discovered that our giant fur ball's life's mission had expanded from love of self & family, to love of ALL.

It is important to our story for you to know that Pie Face has worn a little 2-inch wide bell since his 1st birthday. In the event our son became lost within the eight-acre property, that bell is worn on his collar to help us find him.

Several times each day, Pie Face bounded out the front door and walked with almost dizzying speed, to meet and greet everyone he could find.

Everyone could not help to know when this pup was around, as you could hear that delicate ice cream truck sound long before you saw him. The bell's new effect is that the sound enhanced his persona, as no one could resist the lure. Little children and their dogs oftentimes peer out their apartment windows when they hear his bell, seeking a glimpse of happiness when that bouncing mountain of fur ambles by. They, in turn, call or bark out his name in hopes he will acknowledge their salutations to his presence with a nod or a visit.

Neighbors have said that our son walks ME, which is an accurate observation, as I allow him to pull me in any direction that suits his fancy. I go everywhere he wants within the substantial apartment property and throughout the nearby park. Our local travels start before 7 am and continued intermittently throughout the day, weather permitting.

When we meet someone or their pet who are not comfortable with giant dogs, we accept that it is nothing personal and quickly move on to the next opportunity. Upon receipt of a welcoming word, treat or gesture, my fur ball swiftly walks up close to raise his face, making eye contact while seeking affection.

Pie Face was born with the gift of expression. His cannot hide his feelings and would be a very poor card player, as he is blessed with ear and eyebrow movements. His face seems to have an aura surrounding it, and nearly everyone is made helpless by his charms. People seem paralyzed by the effects of his expressions & wagging tail, and cannot deny this giant Newfoundland his tribute. His overwhelmingly bright aura of caring and unconditional love has led to an ever-expanding cadre of followers, a cult if you will.

The employees of the apartment complex have always showered this Newfoundland pup with a lot of love in the form of special treats. There are the doggie snacks the assistant manager buys with her own money and stores in her desk for "her" dog, and in the form of warm hugs and ear rubs. The office manager is aware that our Newfie is allergic to peanut butter, and she keeps a special stash of very large treats locked near the front door just for our baby.

Pie Face LOVES ear rubs, as proven in his YouTube video: https://www.youtube.com/watch?v=qQ9G2zPvktc .

The warm feelings of apartment staff flow to the maintenance crew. They allow our giant dog to sniff their electric cart for scraps of food and pieces of wood, and frequently talk to him.

When he is not busy walking the miles of sidewalks, seeking attention & food with a keen eye for children and other dogs, he holds court in specific spots that give him a wide view. That view, and a sharp ear makes it certain that he will know of an approaching UPS or FedEx delivery truck. The UPS drivers almost always stop and give treats to the baby, while one UPS driver goes so far as to drop a treat off at our apartment door, even if he was not making a delivery.

There was one unique event where I thought his big brain would shut down from having too much to process. One day in front of our apartment, one FedEx, a UPS and a Post Office van pulled up in rather quick succession. Pie Face's expression was one of amazement and confusion, telegraphing to me a wonder as to whether this is real or not. I could hear the gears turning in his head as he moved it left to right, wondering "just which truck to I go to first?" The process worked its way out as one driver, then another allowed this foodie to run for a treat. Then we went inside to his puppy bed to bask in the glow of what had just transpired.

When he was certain he had gotten all the food they would give him during his apartment office visit, after getting a big drink of water from a reserved bowl from the assistant manager, Pie Face would go outside for round 2. He would hold court in front of the office on the patio, block one traffic lane anywhere it suited him, or fill up a portion of the office sidewalk; laying in wait for affection or food from both residents and vendors.

Pie Face lives for compliments almost as much as he does for food. He will sit up, stand & wag his tail and/or walk over to a stopped vehicle or stroller whenever he hears phrases such as "what a big dog",

By Gene Constant

"beautiful animal", "may I pet him?", "what breed is he?", "does he like treats?", etc. He gets that

treatment from others walking their dogs, as well as from mothers and their babies.

The babies run to Pie Face as if he were a toy or cookie, while some toddlers look from a safe distance (he is SO big!) and say such phrases as "doggie!" and point to him.

During one of our walks in the park, a Eugene police cruiser pulled over, then the cop exited the vehicle for the express purpose of seeing up close and learning more about this amazing Newfie. Speaking of visits to the park, our baby would walk to the playground equipment and lay down, with his head following the movement of toddlers and their mothers in the play area.

Most of the time a mother and baby would come over to talk and touch our gentle giant, and I tell them that Newfoundlands are "nanny" dogs and that it is hard-wired into their brain to love children and for water rescue. When there are kids in the park, you cannot move/motivate him to leave by throwing food for him to chase nor pick him up. His skinny butt stays planted to the earth until he feels a new urge or if the play area is no longer occupied by kids.

And it isn't just toddlers that are attracted to this Oregon bear. Teenagers also give him that rock star attention he so craves, with many young girls asking to touch, talk and pose for pictures with him.

You may be amazed to know that residents go out of their way to feed this man. Rarely does a day go by when a resident sees where we are resting, then walks up and asks us to wait where we are while they go back to their apartment for a saved treat.

Our fur ball almost never barks unless another dog hurts his feelings or if he is inside when a driver is passing by. When in the apartment, the approach of what he absolutely knows to be the sound of a package delivery vehicle will cause him to bark loudly. He wants them to know that he is home and for them not to forget him!

I carry a cushion with pockets that I named "Puppy's Diaper Bag". The pockets hold a towel that others can use to wipe puppy drool off their hands and clothes after a visit, as well as three plastic bags to pick up poop. The cushion makes sitting more comfortable for me when we are camped in a lane of traffic within the complex, and to keep my butt dry while sitting in wet grass.

Ever since we moved to an apartment and started spending more time away from a computer, telephone, clock, calendar or television with my son; I could feel my love for this biggest baby grow. I discovered that a bond could be made stronger by the absence of meaningless distractions.

Whenever we are alone to ourselves, I massage his chest (he LOVES that!), rub his butt, his little puppy ears and that space in between his eyes. I also massage his neck as he listens while I talk, sharing my feelings of affection so that he knows that I love him. Several times a day I remind him that he is mommy's & daddy's boy, that no matter how big he gets he will always be my baby, and that I will always love him.

Then us two dogs just sit outside, soaking up the Oregon weather, basking in the glow that such a close bond fuels. Being semi-retired since 2012 I have had the great fortune to have the time to share a lot of affection, a bromance if you will, with this big man, one that I find to be without equal, to be priceless.

Available for sale at Amazon.com

Birthdays

Puppy has many loves and one of them is our ritual and result from cooking on the grill. His eyebrows rise, his ears perk as he telegraphs feelings of excitement, looking intently at me, seeking confirmation that this is another dream about to come true whenever he heard me say "do you want to bar b cue?" His response is to leap to all four feet and twirl excitedly as we both make our way to the patio door. He next move is oftentimes be to lay and/or sit near that grill until cooked food is served.

We improved the back patio by adding a grass carpet and a short fence. The fence allows for our son to be outside without a leash, giving the two of us a place to hang out in private.

We make a special event that incorporates the arrival of Springtime in Oregon with the celebration of two birthdays. Christina's birthday is on March 14, while Pie's is on March 11.

Ever since his 3rd birthday party we have always cooked a well-done T-bone steak for the birthday boy. And what is a birthday without cake?

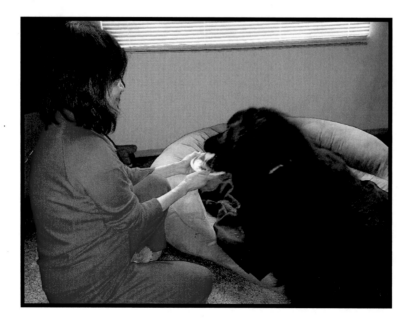

Is it done yet? I am patiently waiting!

Car Rides

Mention the phrase "car ride" around our 4-legged boy and you will see and then be sucked into a whirlwind of excitement, as he would proceed to run in circles, streaking back and forth from me to the door, while I struggle to find his collar to hook his leash, then risk life & limb as he pulls with every bit of strength to the car at the speed of light.

I marvel in knowing that neither of us suffered anything more than a bruise during this unavoidable & unstoppable spectacle of joy. I know that most dogs seem to have been born with a positive-instinctual response, when realization that they are moments from the thrill of air rushing into their face and their fur as the breeze hits them, fueled by anticipation that nose candy to feed their starving brain is mere nanoseconds away.

Once in the back seat, our baby boy fusses from wanting to stick his head out the left, then the right window; and then to perch on the center console, then back to the windows, etc. An advantage of a car ride is that he can share love with new people. It is quite common for people to point while smiling at that giant head of his sticking out and for others to shout compliments to him while waiting for a traffic light to change to green. As a foodie, he can count on treats from the teller at US Bank or at the Westside car wash on 11th Street.

A common ailment with giant dogs, including

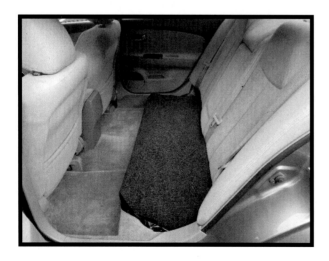

Newfoundlands is hip dysplasia. Pie Face was diagnosed with having this problem by his third birthday. We minimize discomfort and mobility issues by changing the back seat to reduce his need to jump in & out of the car, and by frequent exams at VCA Westmoreland Animal Hospital with changes in medicine as needed. The veterinarian who developed the procedure for canine hip replacement, treating more than 2,000 dogs with this solution, examined our son twice. On that second visit he told us that Pie Face was not a candidate for hip replacement.

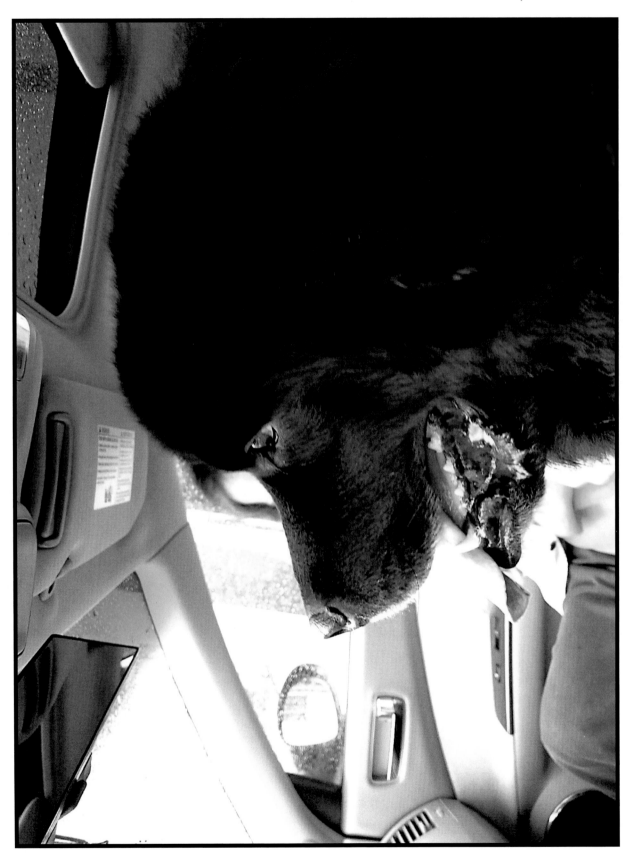

Play time

We both found our baby to be irresistible as a form of entertainment. We have to keep a keen eye out for those strong long arms to prevent a significant injury from those big paws, and nothing but an enjoyable time came from our play. Christina is more gifted than I when it came to use of cardboard and antlers to get his "big baby"

game on.

By Gene Constant

Sleeping

Within our first home, our puppy had the run of the house at night. He had multiple choices from which to rest of which he sampled freely, as he would take charge and walk from one room to the next, never staying to slumber for long in any one spot. He had his embroidered bed in

the

front room, a new bed to share near me in my bedroom, jump into bed with me, or sleep on the leather couch.

The reduced space in our apartment left our son with the option of sleeping in his newest doggie bed, a loose pillow, on my mattress with me or on a rug near the front door.

And so, it came to be as a 60+ year old man, that my snoring was so frequent and loud that I was not fit to sleep with any living creature other than a dog. 😊

My wife would arise in the wee hours of the morning and marvel how Pie Face & my snores seemed to

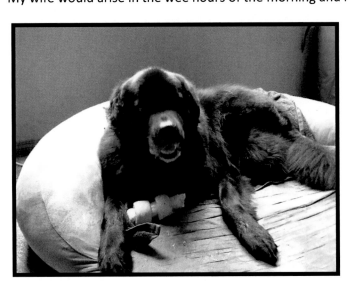

be purposely synchronized, as he would snore, then I would snore, then he would snore, etc., taking turns as it were to sing the song of a pair of tired old dogs.

In this reduced space, the two dogs of the house bonded more closely than most, as I became available to him at any time for more convenient/frequent puppy potty breaks, to trade flatulence, bring a treat, share 3 am walks, someone to cuddle/tickle or just to hang out. "Mr. Personality" learned to slap a paw or to push my mattress whenever he wanted something, or just to be a brat in seeing if I was awake.

January 15, 2018

I awakened at about 6 am to see Pie Face sitting in front of his bed. My first thought was the obvious one in, that I had overslept and that my baby was being too polite to wake me for our early morning bathroom break. As I sat up I could see that he was staring at his bed, where he had recently vomited & then I saw a second pool of vomit on the carpet just near his bed. Christina saw it too and we immediately went to work cleaning up the mess and putting away my bedding.

Our son has always had a sensitive tummy and we are accustomed to being greeted by a pool of yesterday's meals, and where therefore not alarmed by this morning surprise. I got dressed so that he could go outside to pee and reboot for a new day. When we walked to the door, his behavior changed. For the first time ever, he refused to go outside. Knowing that he will do anything for a treat, I gave him a treat after opening the door. He ate the morsel but did not budge. With the door open I tossed another treat past the doorway to the sidewalk. Pie Face walked to the treat, ate it and returned to sit indoors.

Christina made the baby a snack with his daily medicine, which he promptly consumed. For most of the day our puppy continued to sit or lay down near the front door, quietly looking at it. In turn, while sitting in my home office about ten feet away from him, I frequently went to him to pet him and ask if he was ready to go out. He absorbed the love, yet would not budge.

I called VCA Westmoreland Animal Hospital at 8:10 am and was able to get an appointment with his personal doctor, Dr. Bryan Rensema for 4 pm. We did not feel a sense of urgency has he had a history of occasional vomiting, but did not understand his unexpected behavior and made the appointment as a precaution.

Christina fed our pup a small lunch and I continued to return to his side every 15 minutes or so, to encourage him to go potty and to give some love. Pie Face seemed calm and normal otherwise. He laid down on his side, stretched, and made baby noises so that I would rub his paws, ears and chest. Yet not once would he go outside.

At 3:30 pm, our little man was on his feet and racing to the car the very moment when I said, "car ride!" We had not quite made it to Barger Street, when Christina noticed that Pie had fallen to the floor boards of the back-seat area and was stuck. I pulled over where he was able to jump to the street, when he then trotted to the grassy curb and relieved his bladder for the first time that day. He easily jumped onto the back seat after all of that and we traveled to the hospital without further incident. As soon as we got out of the car in the hospital's parking lot, Pie Face made a beeline for a patch of ground whereupon he peed again.

Dr. Resema examined our little Newfie and discussed with us the possibilities. Our dog's pain medicine does list a possible difficulty to pee as a symptom and we had seen that problem to pee before. While his refusal to go outside all day was very troubling, it appeared that he would be his chipper self in no time! When we got home, Pie did pee several times in quick order and walk back into the apartment where the evening progressed as normal. He ate a light meal and I fed him some vanilla ice cream, gave him a lot of loving as he laid down next to our chairs and then his bed, while we intermittently interrupted our television viewing by crawling over to our baby to play with him, or when returning from the kitchen with treats to spoil the lad who had had a long day.

January 16, 2018

At 3 am I awoke to see Pie Face sitting on his butt, looking down at me. I cannot recall if he woke me by hitting my mattress with a paw, or if I sensed that he was staring at me. The apartment was so quiet you could hear a pin drop. While still lying down, I looked up at him and said that we should go outside.

Opposite to his behavior the previous day, Pie Face raced from one side of the driveway separating the apartment buildings to the other, taking a quick pee, sit on his butt, then urgently start running to the next spot in hopes of emptying his bladder.

After almost too many stops to count, he finally seemed satisfied when we got to the car port across the street / next building to our left. He sat, then began to lay down to rest or enjoy the early morning as he so loves to do. Never taking my eyes off him, as the front portion of his body started to touch the asphalt driveway, I heard bone or cartilage break.

My baby instantly got onto his four legs and started to run to the left, towards the apartment complex's office. He stopped to pee two more times and sat again at another carport and waited. A neighbor across from us was on a cigarette break and they knew each other well, so he ran over to her and sat in the carport next to her. I do not remember what we spoke about, but I looked back at my baby boy and suggested to him that it was time to go home.

Our Newfie promptly stood and we trotted back to our apartment, and he returned to his bed. I knelt and petted him, looking into his eyes while telling him how much I loved him and that everything was going to be all right. I rubbed his front legs to reduce their shaking and tried to help him to lay down, but he refused the effort to find comfort. I sensed a certainty that this moment could be dire, and promptly woke Christina up, telling her that "I think his time has come".

She helped me locate the emergency number we keep on the refrigerator door, and I called Emergency Veterinary Hospital in Springfield OR at 4:40 am, telling them that our son may be dying and that we were on our way. While she was getting dressed, Pie Face had quietly moved and sat by the front door near the both of us. I looked down at my outwardly calm child and said, "car ride", whereupon we both ran to the car and raced to the hospital.

Since his arrival via the Portland airport in May 2009, our baby boy has always loved to sit by an open car window, getting some nose candy when he stuck his head out for that fresh Oregon air.

Driving, I sat hoping that what I was seeing & feeling was not real, praying that this nightmare scenario was not taking place, wishing that the doctors could save him from the jaws of death. I glanced over my right shoulder and could see him sitting on his butt at the passenger side of the back seat, looking out the window, but not sticking his nose out for a breeze. I knew that the lifespan of a Newfoundland is 8 to 10 years. My pup was a mere 9-years young, yet I had hoped that he would be immortal.

He was outwardly calm & seemed at peace. He seemed to know.

Instead of seeking me for comfort, as his go-to dad for safety, as he always did when he heard loud noises or when trying to dodge a nurse's thermometer targeting his butt; he was looking away as if he was considering his future.

He was not outwardly agitated, he had not uttered any sound whatsoever this morning, his silence deafening. Not a whimper, not a growl came from this beautiful man to indicate how much stress or pain he was in. I could only hope, as I had the day before, that this would get better in a few moments and a new day would smile of us all.

When we arrived at the hospital at about 4:50 AM. Pie Face turned around, walking on the backseat to the left passenger door and jumped, landing safely on all four paws. The nurse greeted us in the lobby where we sat briefly. I fed my son the last treat I had in my pocket and could not help to notice that he no longer sought my warm embrace nor comfort from what seemed certain to follow.

We spoke to the nurse, who ushered us into a waiting room. She left with our Newfie, then came back carrying a clip board with a form authorizing euthanasia. I looked at the form and then looked at her, saying that while I did say on the phone that perhaps his time had come and may need to be euthanized, that "I have come this morning to save him, not kill him!"

Her response was that the doctor had told her a physical exam was not necessary, as the video image from his jumping out of the car a moment ago was a picture of a dog in great pain and suffering.

She went back to fetch the doctor and our baby boy, and upon entry, the doctor placed his hands over & about puppy's hips and back, pointing out that at his advanced age and pain, we should end his suffering immediately. The doctor said there was no medical option that would comfort him and extend his life.

Pie Face had his face turned away from me the moment the doctor had led our son into the waiting room, his back severely bowed, his expression withdrawn, still not uttering a whine nor whimper. Reflecting upon that moment, I wonder if by his deliberate facing in an opposite direction, that this generous spirit was sparing us both from greater agony than what we were already sharing from the anticipated loss of the other's future comradery and affection.

Not wanting my Newfie to suffer another moment, I signed the permission form and the doctor commenced to inject the first of two medications. The first shot relaxed our baby, whereupon the doctor gave us time to say our good-bye. I was not as stoic as my Newfie, as I cried like a baby, saying repeatedly "my baby, my little baby", all the while combing the fur of his neck and head with my fingers. The second/final shot ended his suffering on this Earth, while perhaps speeding him along to start his new life, a life that he appeared to have been introduced to while taking his last car ride with his mom and dad.

Time of death was 5 AM.

Our big man had died from old age and complications from hip dysplasia.

When my time comes, I hope to be as dignified and accepting of the inevitability of death as he demonstrated. May his passing be a teaching moment for me from which I will know how to inspire others to love as deeply as he did. Humanity can learn a lot from this dog. I know I did.

This book was published not so much to mourn the loss of a life we held precious, but to celebrate the life and joy this puppy brought to us, and hopefully from us to him.

Available for sale at Amazon.com

Once upon a Time...

Once Upon a Time there was a land of endless beauty, where every day was a sunny one, where whispers of clouds lazily floated by as if on parade. It never rained, nor did overly fierce winds disrupt the idyllic pastures and forests.

No one was ever in need for food, nor shelter.

The residents enjoyed eternal life in this place of peace & plenty, where everyone was their friend. They called this paradise Utopia.

Admission to this glorious existence was earned, with entry granted exclusively by the King of Kings. While all present were equals amongst equals; consensus was that One amongst them was uniquely Loved to be elevated to the title of Prince, for they adored him so.

The One accepted the title of Prince with humility, and expressed his appreciation for the high honor by infusing Utopians with his uniquely loving aura, delighting everyone.

By another name, Utopia is known to most as **Heaven**, and the Prince is known to all as **Pie Face**.

As in any delightful story, everyone in Utopia does indeed live **Happily Ever After.**

Mr. Pie Face Constant

2009 - 2018

Beloved son, confidant & friend of Christina & Gene Constant

Pie Face

2009 - 2018

Pie Face, a most beloved Newfoundland 8-year young puppy passed away from complications of hip dysplasia at Emergency Veterinary Hospital in Springfield Oregon at 5 AM January 16, 2018. Doctors said he was in a lot of pain and nothing more could be done to comfort him & prolong his life.

His passing was a few days short of his March 11 birthday when he would have been 9-years old.

Adopted when he was just a 10-week young baby boy by Christina & Gene Constant of Eugene OR, their son resided at Parkside Apartments for several years, where Pie Face's big heart brought such joy and unconditional love to hundreds of Eugene residents.

A fund raiser in Pie Face's honor with the proceeds going to a local animal shelter, will be held Saturday, March 10. Visit www.truetosizeapparel.com/blog/animal-shelter-fundraiser/ for details.

God made Man

Then God made Friend of Man

Angels wings instantly began to flutter, and they hovered over God's newest gift to the Earth, knowing instantly how special this animal was.

A name, they all said in unison, we must give this beautiful creature a name worthy of God's effort.

A reflection of the King of Kings own name was decided to commemorate this wonderful event.

"Yes", they all agreed, "in GOD's mirror image, we shall name him DOG"

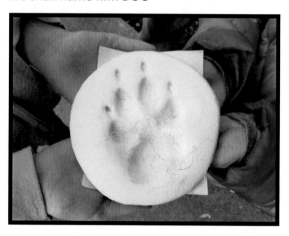

Pie Face's Left paw print, our baby Big Foot 😊

That man could sleep ANYWHERE!

Made in the USA
Middletown, DE
12 September 2018